The
19th Amendment

by Michael Burgan

Content Adviser: Douglas O. Linder, J.D.,
Professor, School of Law,
University of Missouri–Kansas City

Reading Adviser: Rosemary G. Palmer, Ph.D.,
Department of Literacy,
College of Education, Boise State University

COMPASS POINT BOOKS
MINNEAPOLIS, MINNESOTA

Compass Point Books
3109 West 50th Street, #115
Minneapolis, MN 55410

Visit Compass Point Books on the Internet at *www.compasspointbooks.com*
or e-mail your request to *custserv@compasspointbooks.com*

On the cover: Missouri Governor Frederick Gardner as he signs the resolution ratifying the
19th Constitutional Amendment.

Photographs ©: Library of Congress, cover, back cover, 27, 39; Prints Old and Rare, back cover
(far left); Hulton Archive/Getty Images, 5, 11, 16; The Granger Collection, New York, 6, 8, 9, 12,
15, 17, 20, 23; Corbis, 7, 28, 41; North Wind Picture Archives, 13, 26; National Portrait Gallery,
Smithsonian Institution/Art Resource, NY, 14; Stock Montage, Inc., 19, 31; State Archives of
Michigan Research Services, 21; Minnesota Historical Society/Corbis, 24; Bettmann/Corbis, 32,
33, 36, 40; MPI/Getty Images, 34; National Archives and Records Administration, 37.

Managing Editor: Catherine Neitge
Designer/Page Production: Bradfordesign, Inc./Bobbie Nuytten
Photo Researcher: Marcie C. Spence
Cartographer: XNR Productions, Inc.
Educational Consultant: Diane Smolinski
Library Consultant: Kathleen Baxter

Creative Director: Keith Griffin
Editorial Director: Carol Jones

Library of Congress Cataloging-in-Publication Data
Burgan, Michael.
  The 19th Amendment / by Michael Burgan.
     p. cm.—(We the people)
  Includes bibliographical references and index.
  ISBN 0-7565-1260-3 (hardcover)
  1. Women—Suffrage—United States—History—Juvenile literature. 2. United States.
Constitution. 19th Amendment—History—Juvenile literature. I. Title: Nineteenth
Amendment. II. Title.
  KF4895.Z9B78 2005
  324.6'23'0973—dc22   2005002469

TABLE OF CONTENTS

A LONG STRUGGLE ENDS

The year 1917 was a tough one for U.S. President Woodrow Wilson. World War I was raging in Europe. The president had hoped to keep the United States out of the conflict. By April, however, he realized that was impossible. German submarines were attacking U.S. ships, and Wilson asked Congress to declare war.

Wilson also faced a problem at home. Female pickets had been marching in front of the White House nearly every day. The women were demanding their right to vote.

The idea of giving women suffrage—the right to vote—was not new. Suffragists had organized during the 1840s and held the first women's rights convention at Seneca Falls, New York, in 1848. Starting in 1869, some territories and states did let women vote.

Beginning in 1910, suffragists held parades and rallies demanding that all U.S. women citizens be allowed

4

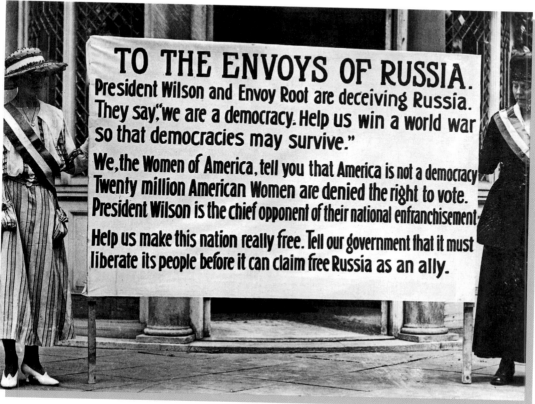

Two women display a protest banner at the White House gates in 1917.

to vote. In 1915, the National American Woman Suffrage Association published an article with 12 reasons why women should vote. The first reason was, "Because those who obey the laws should help to choose those who make the laws." At that time, men alone were making laws that affected women in their roles as mothers and workers.

Suffragists marched and rode horses in a 1913 parade in Washington, D.C.

American ideals of equality and democracy
demanded that women have a say in choosing the people
who made those laws. After all, in 1776, the American
colonists had rebelled against British rule because they had
no voice in their government. Yet more than 100 years later,
American men were denying women that same voice.

Suffragists wanted an amendment to the U.S. Constitution that would let women vote in any election in the United States. Suffragist leaders first proposed an amendment in 1878. But most of the men who ran the national government opposed it. They believed women should not be involved in politics. Their main duties were to be wives and mothers.

Suffrage headquarters in Cleveland, Ohio

By the beginning of 1918, suffragists convinced President Wilson to support the amendment. The U.S. House of Representatives also supported it. But the U.S. Senate did not approve the amendment until 1919. Then, at least 36 states also had to approve the amendment. In 1920, the 19th Amendment finally became law.

It states: "The right of citizens of the United States to vote shall not be denied or abridged by the United States or by any State on account of sex. Congress shall have power to enforce this Article by appropriate legislation."

After decades of struggle, American women had won the most basic right of a democratic society: the right to vote.

8

A 1920 cartoon was entitled "The End of the Climb."

EXPECTED TO OBEY

The struggle for women's suffrage had deep roots. Laws in Great Britain and its American colonies placed women under the control of men. Men expected women to keep silent on important issues and obey their wishes.

In North America, many of these laws and customs remained in place after the colonies won their independence. Single women were expected to do

For many years, women were expected to care for the household and nothing more.

9

whatever their father or other male relatives said. In most cases, women could not sign contracts or work outside the home. When a woman married, any property she owned became her husband's. Most women had little schooling, since their job was to find a husband and raise a family. In the 1700s, one English father wrote to his daughters, "If you happen to have any learning, keep it a profound secret."

Some interpretations of the Bible led to many of the ideas about a woman's role in life during that era. According to Genesis, the first book of the Bible, God created Adam first. So man was seen as more important. Eve was created to be Adam's helper, not his equal. So men were viewed as stronger and more intelligent than women. God gave women their own gifts, however. They were seen as more loving and innocent than men.

Religious leaders claimed that because of these differences, women should give up their rights. Men, in turn, had a duty to provide food for women, build homes,

In the early years of Christianity, St. Paul preached that women could not be church leaders.

and keep them safe. Religious leaders also quoted parts of
the Bible that described what a woman could or could not
do. St. Paul, an early Christian leader, said women should
not speak out in church. Most men thought this meant
women should not speak in public on any important issue.

11

ABOLITION AND EQUALITY

By the end of the 1700s, some women began to talk about equal rights. They wanted women to be able to get an education and have the same legal rights as men. At the same time, the movement to ban slavery in the United States was taking hold.

Many abolitionists were Quakers who believed all races of people were equal in God's eyes. White people had no right to enslave African-Americans. Quakers also said

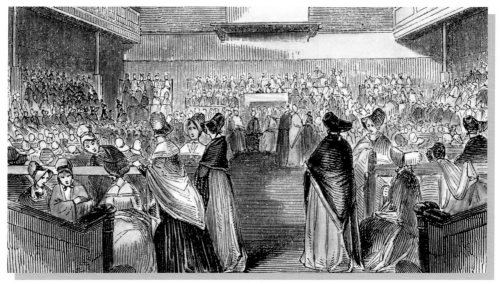

Women were allowed to participate fully in the Quaker church.

that men and women were equal. Among the major religions in the United States, only the Quakers let women speak in church and be leaders.

Many of the women who helped to start the women's movement for equal rights were abolitionists. Sarah and Angelina Grimké, sisters from the slaveholding state of South Carolina, moved to Philadelphia during the 1820s. There in the North, they fought to end slavery. At times, however, male leaders in the abolitionist movement did not want them to speak in public. These men accepted the old ideas about when and where women should speak. Angelina did not agree with these ideas. "If we surrender

Angelina Grimké

13

the right to speak in public this year," she said in 1838, "we must surrender the right to petition next year, and the right to write the year after, and so on."

As more women joined the abolitionist movement, they saw that few men considered them equal. More and more of the women believed they should also fight for women's rights while they continued to battle slavery.

In 1848, Lucretia Mott and Elizabeth Cady Stanton led what Stanton later called a "public meeting for protest and discussion." The meeting was held

Lucretia Mott

that July in Seneca Falls, New York. It was the first women's convention ever held in the United States. It marked the formal start of the women's movement for equal rights. At the convention, Stanton said, "We are assembled … to declare our right to be as free as man is free, to be represented in the government which we are taxed to support."

Stanton also wrote a paper that she based on the Declaration of Independence. In 1776, colonial leaders had written that document to declare the American colonies' independence from Great Britain. In her declaration, Stanton called for a woman's right to vote. Her husband and Lucretia Mott told her she should not mention suffrage. They knew most Americans would oppose the idea. Stanton insisted that the only way women could gain any rights was with the vote.

Elizabeth Cady Stanton

SLOW PROGRESS

After the Seneca Falls convention, women held similar meetings in other states. Many also continued to fight slavery. During the Civil War (1861–1865), Stanton and Susan B. Anthony collected signatures on petitions asking Congress to free the slaves. In 1865, Congress ratified the 13ᵗʰ Amendment to the Constitution, which ended slavery

Susan B. Anthony (left) and Elizabeth Cady Stanton were lifelong friends.

in the United States. In the years to come, amendments were ratified to protect the legal rights of African-Americans and grant them suffrage. Stanton, Anthony, and other women were crushed when lawmakers refused to give women the right to vote as well.

In 1868, Anthony called for an amendment to give women the right to vote. The next year, she and Stanton formed the National Woman Suffrage Association (NWSA).

A meeting of the National Woman Suffrage Association

Later that year, another suffrage association formed, the American Woman Suffrage Association, which was led by Lucy Stone.

Both groups had the same goal, but they saw different ways to reach it. Stanton and Anthony took on other issues besides suffrage. They wanted better treatment for women in the workplace and the home, and better education. Stone and her group wanted to focus solely on suffrage. They were afraid they might lose support if they spoke about too many issues.

Finally, in 1878, the NWSA found a member of Congress willing to support women's suffrage. Anthony wrote the proposed amendment to the Constitution, which said, "The right of citizens of the United States to vote shall not be denied ... by the United States or by any state on account of sex." Many women signed petitions supporting the proposed amendment.

Many men, however—and some women—opposed the suffrage amendment. People who disagreed with the

aims of the women's movement were sometimes called
anti-suffragists or antis. One of their leaders was
Madeleine Dahlgren. She spoke against the suffrage
amendment in the U.S. Senate. Women did not need the
right to vote, she said, since "each family is represented
through its head"—the father. When women sought their
own vote, she said, they risked breaking the unity of the
family. Some male lawmakers who opposed women's
suffrage pointed to the antis' views to support their own
rejection of the amendment.

Marchers who disagreed with the anti-suffragists carried a banner in a 1914 parade.

SUCCESS IN THE WEST

By the time the suffrage amendment was introduced in Congress, a small number of American women already had the right to vote. In the American West, settlers were moving into regions called territories. Citizens created their own territorial governments before becoming a state.

In 1869, Wyoming became a U.S. territory, and that same year the governor signed a law granting women the right to vote. The Utah territory gave women that right in 1870.

Wyoming women could vote in 1869.

During the 1890s, both Wyoming and Utah became states, and they continued to support women's suffrage. Other Western states also granted women suffrage— Colorado in 1893 and Idaho in 1896. In other states, however, most male voters did not seem interested in giving women this right.

To try to strengthen the women's movement, the two main suffrage groups joined together. In 1890, they formed the National American Woman Suffrage Association (NAWSA). Other women's organizations and more African-American women also joined the fight to vote. One of the most famous African-American suffragists was Sojourner Truth.

Sojourner Truth

A former slave, Truth spoke often for women's suffrage. In one speech, she told men, "You have been having our rights so long, that you think, like a slave-holder, that you own us."

During the 1890s, Ida B. Wells-Barnett was another well-known black suffragist. A journalist and community activist, she started black women's clubs in Illinois. She founded the first African-American women's suffrage organization, the Alpha Suffrage Club of Chicago.

Some white women, however, opposed the black suffragists. They feared that racists would block women's suffrage if black women could vote. Some suffragist leaders only wanted "educated, intelligent white women" to vote. Other suffragists complained that "ignorant" immigrant men could vote, but the most intelligent white women could not. At that time, many white Americans looked down on people from different races or backgrounds.

Ida B. Wells

25

Black Heritage USA

The image of Ida B. Wells-Barnett appeared on a stamp in 1989.

ON THE STREETS

Suffragist leaders continued to seek out members of Congress who supported their cause. Year after year, the suffrage amendment was introduced in Congress. Each time, it was defeated. But starting in 1910, more states began giving women the right to vote. These included Washington, Oregon, California, Kansas, and Arizona.

Suffrage supporters met in Winfield, Kansas, in 1910.

At the same time, however, voters in Northeastern, Midwestern, and Southern states rejected women's suffrage.

By this time, women had gained other rights. They could go to college—something that had been denied to most women in the past. Women also had more independence. Several million worked outside the home. But there was still much work to be done. A few members of the women's movement wanted to take more direct action.

In 1910, the Women's Political Union (WPU) held the nation's first major suffragist parade. The leader was Harriot Stanton Blatch, the daughter of Elizabeth Cady Stanton. Blatch organized a number of parades, some with 10,000 women marching for their rights. Blatch wrote, "The enemy must see women, marching in increasing numbers year by year … holding high their banners, Votes for Women."

Since Blatch lived in New York, her first concern was winning suffrage for women in that state. In December 1912,

Suffragists gathered for a 1912 parade in New York.

she led a group of marchers from New York City to
Albany, the state capital. The walk took almost two
weeks. The women often stopped to build fires to warm
themselves. They also talked to everyone they met about
women's rights.

Another suffragist leader, Alice Paul, copied Blatch.
In 1913, Paul organized the first major suffragists' parade
in Washington, D.C. About 8,000 marchers filled the
streets. On the sidewalks, several thousand men shouted

insults at the women, and some attacked the marchers. Washington, D.C., police could not control the crowds, and more than 200 women were injured. Many Americans were outraged at the way the women were treated and impressed by their bravery.

Women's suffrage had the support of working women. They had formed their own unions to help them get higher pay and improve their working conditions.

Thousands of suffragists marched in Washington, D.C.

27

Female union members saw that winning the right to vote was another way to better their lives. If they could vote, they could elect lawmakers who would support their concerns.

Women also had support from a new political group, the Progressive Party. The Progressives, led by former President Theodore Roosevelt, wanted to use government to help people who did not always receive fair treatment. Many Progressives backed the suffrage movement.

28

Theodore Roosevelt (center) and his fellow Progressives supported women's suffrage.

KEY BATTLES

For many years, the National American Woman Suffrage Association had focused on getting each state to give women suffrage. But by 1915, the women realized this strategy took too long. They also realized that some states would never let women vote. The only answer was to get Congress to pass a constitutional amendment. Then only

Suffragists realized that trying to get women the vote state-by-state took too long.

three-fourths of the states would have to agree to the amendment. And when they did, all states would have to let women vote. The NAWSA decided to do more to pass an amendment.

Carrie Chapman Catt, NAWSA president, began forming "suffrage schools" to teach women about the history of the movement. The students learned how to speak with newspaper reporters and gain new members for the NAWSA. The group soon grew from 100,000 members to more than 2 million members. The schools also taught women how to talk to politicians and lobby for their vote. Catt spent most of her time in Washington, D.C. She tried to win support from President Woodrow Wilson and members of Congress.

Not all suffragists agreed with the NAWSA strategy. Some had more radical ideas. Alice Paul led the women who wanted to take more action. She had spent time in Great Britain, where suffragists were willing to be arrested for their cause. Paul led a group called the Congressional

Union for Woman's Suffrage, which later became the National Woman's Party (NWP). Its members went to states where women could already vote. They tried to convince female voters to support members of the Republican Party. President Wilson was a Democrat, and Paul thought he had not done enough to help women's suffrage.

In January 1917, the NWP started to send pickets to the White House. They carried signs and banners of all sizes. One banner read, "Mr. President, how long must women wait for liberty?" The protests were seen by many

Suffragists protested at the White House in 1917.

31

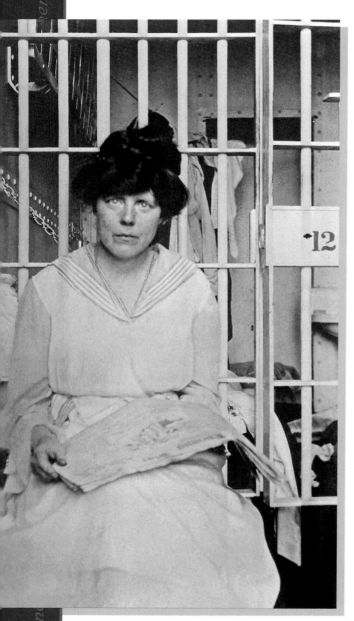

Suffragist Lucy Burns was arrested and jailed six times.

as unpatriotic since the United States had just entered World War I. At times, some NWP pickets were arrested. The police said they were illegally blocking the sidewalks. Paul claimed the police jailed them for their statements against Wilson and the war.

In jail, some of the pickets protested their arrest by refusing to eat. The police then forced food into their bodies through a long tube down their throats. One woman described how a doctor "forced the tube through my lips and down my throat, I gasping and suffocating with the agony of it."

VICTORY AT LAST

Carrie Chapman Catt and the NAWSA opposed Alice Paul's methods. They continued to support President Wilson through the war. They still believed they would be more successful with persuasion than with public protests. Catt feared the entire suffragist movement would lose support because of the National Woman's Party. Still, the NWP believed its protests were working by bringing great attention to their struggle. During 1917, Congress began to think harder about women's suffrage.

Members of the NAWSA supported President Woodrow Wilson.

33

World War I (1914–1918) may have given the suffragists their biggest boost. After the United States entered the war in 1917, about 5 million American men

A 1918 poster promotes women workers during World War I.

joined the military. Women filled the jobs they left behind, including dangerous ones involving heavy machinery. Women sewed clothes for soldiers, helped make their weapons, and served as doctors and nurses. On January 9, 1918, President Wilson gave his support to what became the 19th Amendment.

The next day, the U.S. House of Representatives voted on the amendment. Two-thirds of the members of the House and Senate must approve an amendment to the Constitution. In the House, women's suffrage won 274 votes—exactly two-thirds. The Senate, however, was less willing to support the amendment.

In September, Wilson spoke to the senators. "We have made partners of the women in this war," he said. "Shall we admit them only to a partnership of sacrifice and suffering and toil, and not to a partnership of privilege and right? This war could not have been fought … if it had not been for the services of women."

But the Senate rejected the women's suffrage

Jeannette Rankin, the first woman to serve in Congress, is presented with the flag that flew at the House of Representatives during passage of the suffrage amendment in 1918.

amendment by just two votes. Many of the opponents believed each state should decide whether its female citizens could vote. A second vote in February 1919 also failed, this time by just one vote. Finally in June, the Senate voted again. This time, 66 senators out of 96 voted for the amendment—two votes more than the necessary

H. J. Res. 1.

Sixty-sixth Congress of the United States of America;

At the First Session,

Begun and held at the City of Washington on Monday, the nineteenth day of May, one thousand nine hundred and nineteen.

JOINT RESOLUTION

Proposing an amendment to the Constitution extending the right of suffrage to women.

Resolved by the Senate and House of Representatives of the United States of America in Congress assembled (two-thirds of each House concurring therein), That the following article is proposed as an amendment to the Constitution, which shall be valid to all intents and purposes as part of the Constitution when ratified by the legislatures of three-fourths of the several States.

"ARTICLE ————.

"The right of citizens of the United States to vote shall not be denied or abridged by the United States or by any State on account of sex.

"Congress shall have power to enforce this article by appropriate legislation."

F. H. Gillett

Speaker of the House of Representatives.

Thos. R. Marshall

Vice President of the United States and
President of the Senate.

The 19th Amendment was approved by the Senate in June 1919.

two-thirds majority. According to one newspaper, the suffragists watching the vote "broke into deafening applause" that lasted for two minutes.

Once Congress approves a constitutional amendment, the lawmakers in three-quarters of the states must also ratify, or approve, it. In 1919, the country had 48 states, so 36 had to approve the amendment for it to become part of the Constitution. Across the nation, suffragists and anti-suffragists scrambled to win support for their views. The suffragists focused on states that already let women vote. But they would also need to convince lawmakers in others states as well.

Within six months of the Senate vote, 22 states gave their approval. By the end of March 1920, the number had risen to 35. Now the last battle was at hand. Several states had already rejected the amendment. The suffragists knew they could not win support in most of the Southern states that had already rejected the amendment and several in New England that had not yet voted. Lawmakers in those states had strongly opposed suffrage for years. Tennessee emerged as the state most likely to ratify the amendment, though the vote would be close.

In mid-August, the Tennessee Senate voted for the 19th Amendment. The state House voted on it on August 18. One of the lawmakers was 24-year-old Harry Burn. He was the youngest member of the House. He had earlier said he would not vote for the amendment unless there was a tie. Burn carried a note from his mother in his pocket. She had told him to be a "good boy" and "vote for suffrage! Don't keep them in doubt."

Missouri Governor Frederick Gardner signed the resolution ratifying the 19th Amendment in 1919. Missouri became the 11th state to ratify the amendment.

39

The vote reached 48 for the amendment and 48 against. Burn then changed his vote from "no" to "yes," and another representative did as well. With the approval of the Tennessee House, all women in the United States finally had the right to vote.

Across the country, suffragists celebrated their victory. And in November 1920, for the first time ever, women in every state voted for the U.S. president. The

Suffragists celebrated the passage of the 19th Amendment in August 1920.

American women could finally cast their ballots in 1920.

next year, Carrie Chapman Catt summed up the work of the NAWSA and other suffragists. She said they had given "to American women an opportunity, a dignity and liberty which in 1848 were a dream in the minds only of a few."

Today, tens of millions of American women vote in every election. Thousands also hold elected government positions. The 19th Amendment guarantees that women will always play an important role in U.S. politics.

41

GLOSSARY

abolitionists—people who supported the banning of slavery

amendment—formal change made to a law or legal document, such as the Constitution

Constitution—the document that describes the basic laws and principles by which the United States is governed

democracy—a form of government in which people elect their leaders

lobby—attempt to influence or sway a public official toward a desired action

petitions—collections of signatures showing support for an issue

pickets—people posted at a site for a demonstration or protest

racists—people who believe one race is better than others

radical—favoring extreme changes or reforms

strategy—a careful plan or method

suffragists—people who favor extending the right to vote, especially to women

DID YOU KNOW?

- The first woman elected to Congress was Jeannette Rankin (1880–1973) of Montana. She served from 1917 to 1919 and from 1941 to 1943, choosing not to seek reelection to the House of Representatives either time. She lost a Senate race in 1918, probably because of her 1917 vote against the United States' entry into World War I. She worked tirelessly for women's rights and world peace.

- The 19th Amendment was sometimes called the Anthony Amendment, since Susan B. Anthony wrote the original statement and worked so hard to make it law.

- An early male supporter of women's suffrage was Frederick Douglass. He was a former slave who became an abolitionist and a writer. He was one of several men to speak at the Seneca Falls convention of 1848.

- In 1920, the National American Woman Suffrage Association ended, and its members formed the League of Women Voters. Its goal was to educate women on important political issues. The League of Women Voters still exists, with groups in all 50 states, Washington, D.C., and the U.S. Virgin Islands.

IMPORTANT DATES

Timeline

1848	Elizabeth Cady Stanton and Lucretia Mott lead the Seneca Falls convention, the first large gathering in the United States to discuss women's rights.
1869	Wyoming grants women the right to vote.
1878	Susan B. Anthony writes the amendment that will grant women suffrage once it becomes part of the U.S. Constitution.
1910	In New York City, the Women's Political Union leads the first large U.S. suffragist parade.
1917	The United States enters World War I; Alice Paul and members of her National Woman's Party are arrested for picketing in front of the White House.
1918	President Woodrow Wilson gives his support to the amendment for women's suffrage, which is now called the 19th Amendment; the U.S. House of Representatives also accepts the amendment, but the U.S. Senate rejects it.
1919	The Senate approves the 19th Amendment.
1920	Tennessee becomes the 36th state to ratify the 19th Amendment, and it officially becomes part of the U.S. Constitution.

IMPORTANT PEOPLE

SUSAN B. ANTHONY (1820–1906)
Author of the original amendment giving women the right to vote

CARRIE CHAPMAN CATT (1859–1947)
President of the National American Woman Suffrage Association

LUCRETIA MOTT (1793–1880)
Early abolitionist and one of the founders of the U.S. women's movement

ALICE PAUL (1885–1977)
Militant suffragist and author of the Equal Rights Amendment

ELIZABETH CADY STANTON (1815–1902)
One of the founders of the U.S. women's movement and a leading suffragist

LUCY STONE (1818–1893)
Newspaper publisher and founder of the American Woman Suffrage Association

SOJOURNER TRUTH (1797?–1883)
Former slave who became an abolitionist and suffragist

IDA B. WELLS-BARNETT (1862–1931)
Journalist and founder of the first African-American suffrage organization

WANT TO KNOW MORE?

At the Library

Bausum, Ann. *With Courage and Cloth: Winning the Fight for a Woman's Right to Vote.* Washington, D.C.: National Geographic, 2004.

Keller, Kristin Thoennes. *Carrie Chapman Catt.* Minneapolis: Compass Point Books, 2006.

Landau, Elaine. *The Abolitionist Movement.* New York: Children's Press, 2004.

Monroe, Judy. *The Nineteenth Amendment: A Woman's Right to Vote.* Springfield, N.J.: Enslow Publishers, 1998.

Sigerman, Harriet. *Elizabeth Cady Stanton: The Right Is Ours.* New York: Oxford University Press, 2001.

On the Web

For more information on the *19th Amendment*, use FactHound to track down Web sites related to this book.

1. Go to *www.facthound.com*

2. Type in a search word related to this book or this book ID: 0756512603

3. Click on the *Fetch It* button.

Your trusty FactHound will fetch the best Web sites for you!

On the Road

National Women's Hall of Fame

76 Fall St.

Seneca Falls, NY 13148

315/568-8060

To learn about extraordinary women and view exhibits in the town where the women's movement began

The Susan B. Anthony House

17 Madison St.

Rochester, NY 14608

585/235-6124

To visit the home of one of the leading crusaders for women's rights in the United States

Look for more We the People books about this era:

The Dust Bowl

Ellis Island

The Great Depression

Navajo Code Talkers

Pearl Harbor

The Persian Gulf War

The Statue of Liberty

The Titanic

The Tuskegee Airmen

A complete list of We the People titles is available on our Web site:
www.compasspointbooks.com

INDEX

About the Author

Michael Burgan is a freelance writer of books for children and adults. A history graduate of the University of Connecticut, he has written more than 90 fiction and nonfiction children's books for various publishers. For adult audiences, he has written news articles, essays, and plays. Michael Burgan is a recipient of an Educational Press Association of America award.